Oxford Reading Tree

Read at Home
Handbook
Helping your child to read

Kate Ruttle and Annemarie Young

OXFORD
UNIVERSITY PRESS

Contents

Read at Home and learning to read

What is Read at Home?

Read at Home features all the familiar *Oxford Reading Tree* characters in 30 exciting adventures written especially for you to enjoy with your child at home. The stories are carefully graded across five levels (from 'Getting Ready to Read' to 'Reading with Confidence') and within each level there is gradual progression from Book A to Book C. The *Read at Home* levels are also linked to the *Oxford Reading Tree* stages.

Each *Read at Home* story contains:

◎ Practical tips and stimulating ideas for you to use with your child when reading and discussing the story.

◎ Puzzles and activities to encourage children to look for detail and practise wider reading skills.

◎ A 'Useful common words' panel to highlight high frequency words used in the story, which children will be learning at school.

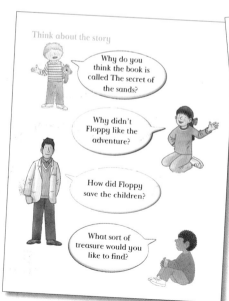

Think about the story

Why do you think the book is called The secret of the sands?

Why didn't Floppy like the adventure?

How did Floppy save the children?

What sort of treasure would you like to find?

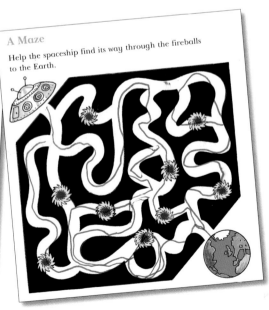

A Maze

Help the spaceship find its way through the fireballs to the Earth.

Age	Read at Home Level	Oxford Reading Tree Stage

Getting Ready to Read

3-4 years	Level 1	Stages 1- 1+

Starting to Read

4 years	Level 2	Stages 2-3

Becoming a Reader

4-5 years	Level 3	Stages 3-4

Building Confidence

5-6 years	Level 4	Stages 4-5

Reading with Confidence

6-7 years	Level 5	Stages 5-7

For more information on Read at Home go to www.oxfordchildrens.co.uk

Getting children ready for reading

Our aim in this handbook is to show you how you can help your child from an early age so that learning to read is successful and enjoyable for you both.

In the early stages of learning to read children need to develop skills at the different levels. We can help them do this by reading with them and by:

- talking about stories and using story language

- using clues in the pictures to help them to understand the story

- helping them to recognise common words by sight so that they aren't having to struggle to work out all of the words in a sentence

- developing a knowledge of 'phonics' (how sounds are represented by individual letters and combinations of letters)

- using the 'context' (what comes before and after a word in the sentence or paragraph) to help make sense of the story.

Listening to stories

From the time they are babies, you can help children to become readers by:

- ◎ sharing your enjoyment of books
- ◎ reading stories and talking about the pictures
- ◎ comparing events in books with your own shared experiences
- ◎ pointing out signs and logos when you go shopping
- ◎ teaching them nursery rhymes and songs.

These simple activities help to prepare children for reading.

Starting to Read

When your child starts paying attention to the printed words in the book you are reading to them, they may be ready to start learning to read.

- ◎ Try to make time to read with your child every day.

- ◎ Read favourite stories again and again. Children love this.

- ◎ Build confidence by reading lots of books at the same reading level, and continue to re-read earlier books. If you push children to read books that are too hard, they are likely to lose interest.

Most important of all, if you are relaxed and enjoy reading with your child, that will pass on very strong messages about what fun reading is.

(1) (3–4-year olds)

Level 1: Getting Ready to Read

How to support your child at this stage

Reading and enjoyment

Before they begin to join in with reading, children need to listen to stories, songs and rhymes, to join in with the telling of familiar stories, to handle books and enjoy looking at pictures. Be guided by their interests.

What skills do children need?

When they are at the 'Getting Ready to Read' stage of *Read at Home*, children can:

- ◎ enjoy sharing and talking about books

- ◎ recognise their own name

- ◎ match some words (for example, match *Mum* from a set of cards to the word *Mum* in a sentence)

- ◎ recognise some letter sounds (for example, some of the sounds in their name).

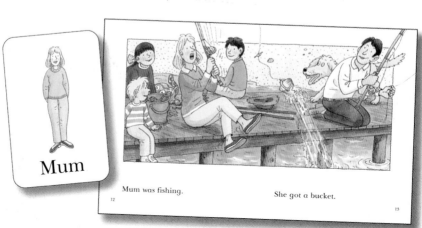

Mum

Mum was fishing.

12

She got a bucket.

13

Some of the activities on page 12 will help to develop many of the skills children need in order to begin reading. At this early level, children's reading relies on the following:

- **Motivation** – if your child is inquisitive about how reading works, they will find the process much more interesting.

- **Memory** – don't be concerned if your child seems to be memorising rather than reading the book (and **please** don't cover up the pictures). Memory is a key skill for reading.

- **Concentration** – most children won't be ready to read until they can sustain concentration for 5–10 minutes.

- **Seeing and hearing** – in order to recognise individual words and letters in reading, children need to be good at identifying things that are the same or different.

Practical tips

Read with your child as often as you can: on the bus, in the bath, and in bed at night when you can make it special. Use the bedtime story as an opportunity to read *to* your child – they are usually too tired to read *with* you at that time.

Understanding print – story and meaning

Before you read a story with your child:

- talk about the title and the pictures on the cover

- look through the pictures together

- discuss what you think the story might be about.

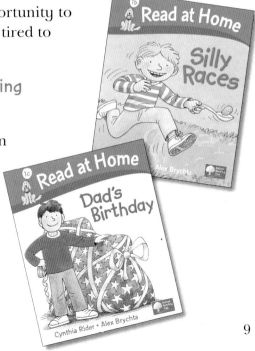

Read the story to your child. (It's not cheating!)

◎ Don't stop to talk on the first read through.

◎ Point to the words as you read, matching one spoken word to one written word.

He got a boot.

Re-read the story with your child, encouraging them to join in with repeated phrases.

◎ Talk about the pictures and discuss what's going to happen next.

When you have finished reading, ask questions like:

◎ *What was your favourite bit?*

◎ *Why do you think Floppy fell into the water?*

◎ *Has this ever happened to you?*

There are suggested 'Think about the story' questions at the end of all the *Read at Home* books to help develop discussion and understanding.

Understanding print – words and letters

When you have read the story, you can then start to draw attention to the words and letters.

- Check that your child knows where to start reading and that the print is read from left to right.

- Draw attention to the starting sound of a word and then ask them to find another word beginning with the same letter sound.

- Ask them to find two words that are the same.

In all of the *Read at Home* books, there is a list of common useful words used in the book. (For a full list see page 29.) This shouldn't be used as a vocabulary test, but to help you when you are looking for other books your child might enjoy reading.

Brian Wildsmith
Cat on the Mat

More ideas for reading at this level

Read as many books as you can, including:

- retellings of traditional tales and fairy stories

- familiar nursery rhymes

- alphabet books

- catalogues (Children love recognising things in them!)

- classic books, like *Each Peach Pear Plum* by Alan and Janet Ahlberg and the *Cat on the Mat* books by Brian Wildsmith. Your local library will be able to help you.

Games and activities

Improve memory and concentration by playing simple card and board games, for example, snap and lotto.

Story activities

◎ Talk about the books you are reading.

◎ Encourage children to retell favourite stories.

◎ Take your child to the library and encourage them to make choices about the books they want to read.

Picture activities

Find the feather hidden in every picture.

◎ Develop observation skills with, for example, the 'Find the … hidden' activities in the *Read at Home* books.

◎ Talk about the extra details in the pictures. *Read at Home* stories usually include hidden bones and glasses and lots of visual jokes.

"Get that hat," said Kipper.   Biff ran.

Word activities

◎ Reading for meaning: look for words, signs and logos when you are out and about.

◎ Word building: use magnetic letters on the fridge and sponge letters in the bath.

◎ Use the *Read at Home Flashcards Word Games*.

Phonics activities

Encourage your child to recognise letters and rhymes.

◎ Recite rhymes they know, like *1, 2, 3, 4, 5, once I caught a fish…*, and get them to supply the rhyming word.

(4-year olds)

Level 2: Starting to Read

How to support your child at this stage

Reading and enjoyment

When you read aloud, include some books which are only slightly too hard for your child so that they can soon begin to read them.

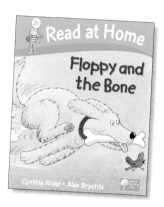

Introduce paired reading, where you and your child read aloud together from the same familiar book. You can read more quietly as they become more confident.

What skills do children need?

When they are at the 'Starting to Read' stage of *Read at Home*, children are continuing to develop and refine all the skills from Level 1. They should also be learning to:

◉ recognise a few common words by sight (for example, *said*)

◉ retell a simple story

◉ read a simple sentence using pictures to help

◉ recognise some letter sounds at the beginning of words (for example the 'd' in *dog*).

Practical tips

Always read a book aloud before you ask your child to read the book to you. This gives them the chance to understand the story, and to hear the words and language patterns.

Understanding print – story and meaning

◎ Talk about the title and cover pictures to predict what the story might be about.

◎ Point to the words as you read, matching one spoken word to one written word.

◎ Talk about what's happening and what will happen next.

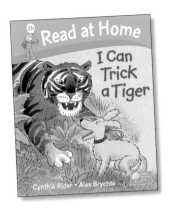

When you have finished reading, ask questions like:

◎ *What was your favourite bit?*

◎ *Why did the tiger let Floppy go?*

There are suggested 'Think about the story' questions at the end of all the *Read at Home* books to help develop discussion and understanding.

Understanding print – words and letters

Play word- and letter-spotting games like these with your child:

◎ *Can you find Floppy's name on this page?*

◎ *Can you find something in the picture that begins with the sound 'b'?*

More ideas for reading at this level

Read as many books as you can, including:

◎ retellings of traditional tales and fairy stories (for example, Aesop's *The Dog and the Bone*)

◎ familiar nursery rhymes (for example, *Nonsense Nursery Rhymes* by Richard Edwards)

◎ classic books, like *The Hungry Caterpillar* by Eric Carle.

Games and activities

Teach your child to recognise their own name, family names and family words like Mum and Dad.

Story activities

- Ask children to draw pictures of their favourite storybook or TV characters and to talk about them.

- Invent new adventures for the characters together.

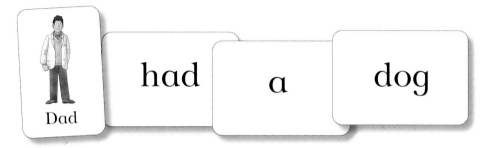

Dad   had   a   dog

Picture activities

- Use sequences of pictures to tell stories.

- Talk about what a picture is 'about' to help your child to recognise the important elements.

- Play 'How many can you see?' games.

Word activities

- Use the *Read at Home Flashcards Word Games* to play:

  - Snap (matching a limited number of words)

  - Memory game: turning over pairs of cards to find two that match.

- Look for words, signs and logos in the environment around you (restaurant names, shops, high street brands, 'P' for 'Parking', TV programmes and characters).

15

Phonics activities

- Play games like:

  – Sound sets: finding sets of words which begin or end with the same sound.

  – Letter trains: making chains of words, matching the last letter of one with the first letter of the next.

- Play games like 'I spy with my little eye something beginning with 'a''.

- Sing the alphabet song.

- Play alliterative games, like 'Annie got an apple, Ben got a bike', etc.

- Use magnetic letters to make words. Copy words from the flashcards, rather than sounding out whole words.

- Use modelling clay or playdough to make letter shapes.

- Find pictures in magazines to make sets of 'Words which begin with…' and make an alphabet scrapbook.

3

(4–5-year olds)

Level 3: Becoming a Reader

How to support your child at this stage

Reading and enjoyment

When you read aloud, encourage your child to look at the words and pictures with you.

With paired reading (see page 13), let your child set the speed. When they hesitate, begin to say the first sound of the tricky word to help them.

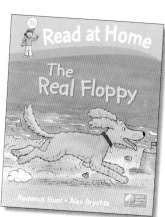

What skills do children need?

When they are at the 'Becoming a Reader' stage of *Read at Home*, children still need to practise all the skills from the earlier levels. They should also be starting to:

◈ recognise 10–20 common words by sight

◈ read simple sentences

◈ recognise all the letter sounds at the beginning of words

◈ use some expression when they re-read books.

Practical tips

◈ Look at the pictures together before you read, discussing what you think the story might be about.

"Look at that," said Dad.
"Dogs can't go on the sand."

"Poor Floppy!" said Mum.
"I'll take him for a walk."

10

11

17

- Read aloud any words that might be tricky.
- Read any repeated phrases. This will help your child recognise them when they read the book on their own.

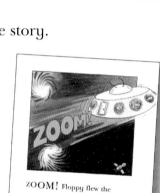

Understanding print – story and meaning

Continue with all the earlier activities.

- Talk about all the events in the story: *What happened first? Then what happened? What happened in the end?*
- Help them to talk about their feelings about the story.

If your child loses the meaning of what they are reading, ask them to stop and think about what the word or sentence might mean, using a variety of strategies:

ZOOM! Floppy flew the spaceship out of danger. "Phew! Just in time," he said.

- reading to the end of the sentence and then deciding on a sensible word to fill the gap
- re-reading the sentence
- using the picture
- using the letter sounds.

If they still can't read the word, read it for them.

Understanding print – words and letters

- Point out letters that go together, for example, *th, sh.*
- Draw your child's attention to speech marks, punctuation, sound effects and action words (for example, *BUMP, ZOOM*).

Read as many books as you can at a similar reading level.

Continue to play the games and activities suggested for Levels 1 and 2, and introduce these new skills.

Story activities

◎ Talk about what might happen after the story ending.

◎ Together, write captions for photographs to provide a motivating and personal book.

◎ Introduce simple non-fiction books, so your child can see that books have many different purposes.

◎ Introduce simple rhyme books (for example, *Dr Seuss*).

> Where do spaceships go in space? Where would you like to go?

Picture activities

◎ Make up your own story to go with wordless books like *The Snowman* by Raymond Briggs.

Word activities

Use *Read at Home Flashcards Word Games* to play games:

◈ Choose two or more words from a selection. Can your child say a sentence containing those words?

◈ Write a sentence, but miss out one word. Can they choose a word that could fill the gap from a set of words?

◈ Give them a page from a magazine. How many common words like *but, come, want,* etc. can they recognise?

Phonics activities

◈ When you play *I spy*, include words that begin with two consonants, for example, *br, cl, dr, st*; words that end with two consonants, for example, *nd, st, lk*; or words that rhyme.

◈ Use magnetic letters. Build a word and ask your child to make a word that rhymes, or is one letter different, or begins or ends with the same letter.

◈ Show your child one of the flashcard words. How many times can they write it in one minute?

(5–6-year olds)

Level 4: Building Confidence in Reading

How to support your child at this stage

Reading and enjoyment

Try sharing a book together – you read one page and your child reads the next. This has three main advantages:

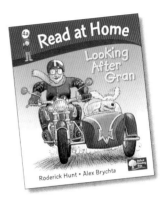

- You are modelling what fluent reading sounds like.

- The book is completed more quickly, and your child is more likely to want to re-read it.

- If your child loses the meaning of the story while they concentrate on reading their pages, they can pick up the meaning again while you are reading.

What skills do children need?

When children are Building Confidence in Reading (Level 4) they still need to practise all the skills from the earlier levels. They should also be learning to:

- recognise 30–50 common words by sight

- read harder sentences, with less support

- use letter sounds to help make words

- recognise more words in sentences.

Understanding print — story and meaning

Children who are reading at this stage should be
encouraged to:

◎ re-read the text when it doesn't make sense

◎ work out tricky words, using meaning and
pictures as well as phonics

◎ make links between events in books and
their own lives (*I remember when…*)

◎ use expression when re-reading a text.

Understanding print — letters and words

◎ Help children to focus on chunks in words, rather
than individual letter sounds, for example *camp/ing*.

◎ When your child is stuck on a word, help
them to:

The family went camping. They
put up a tent.

     –   sound out chunks of the word

     –   re-read the sentence to create a
          meaningful context

     –   read on to the end of the sentence.

Read as many books as you can at
this level. The more children read,
the more confident and successful
they will become as readers.

Continue to play the games and activities suggested for the earlier levels, and introduce these new skills.

Story activities

◈ Encourage your child to write their own short stories with your help.

◈ Ask them to think think about how characters might feel and what they might think at different times in the story.

◈ Ask your child to retell stories from TV programmes and films you have watched.

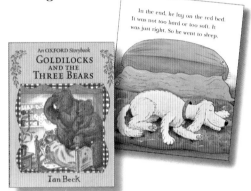

Picture activities

◈ Encourage your child to 'read' the pictures in books they can't yet read. How much can they find out? Can they produce their own version of the story?

Word activities

◈ Make jumbled words. For example, cut out the letters from a word like *some* and ask your child to rebuild the word.

◈ Build vocabulary: *I went shopping and I got an amazing anteater; a beautiful bike; colourful crayons,* etc. (alliterative adjectives).

Phonics activities

◈ Start pointing out tricky words which you can't sound out.

  – Which words look as if they should rhyme, but don't? For example, *home, come; do, no.*

  – Which words rhyme, even though they look different? For example, *come, sum; there, bear, hair.*

(6–7-year olds)

Level 5: Reading with Confidence

How to support your child at this stage

Reading and enjoyment

At this level continue to find time to read together (page 21) and also continue to read *to* your child. When you read a story to your child you are:

◎ Sharing the joy of books, stories, picture, poems and information. Your enthusiasm for books will rub off on your child.

◎ Sharing and creating a story world that you can enjoy together. This story world is a safe and reassuring place which develops a bond between the two of you.

◎ Demonstrating what good reading aloud sounds like.

What skills do children need?

When children are Reading with Confidence (Level 5), they should be able to:

◎ recognise 50+ words and use a range of strategies to work out unknown words

◎ express opinions about the characters and story

◎ read silently and begin to read ahead

◎ begin to attempt longer books.

Understanding print – story and meaning

Children who are reading at this level should be encouraged to:

- sounds out longer and more difficult words
- read a story they have read before with some expression
- talk about what happens in the book
- self-correct and make meaning as they read
- express opinions about the book, the characters and the plot. Allow them to tell you if they don't like a book and why – explain that it's OK not to like some books if they don't get pleasure out of them.

Understanding print – letters and words

- Help children to focus on chunks in words, rather than individual letter sounds for example, *bark/ed.*
- When your child is stuck on a word, help them to:
  - sound out chunks of the word
  - re-read the sentence to create a meaningful sentence
  - read on to the end of the sentence.

Read as many books as you can and continue to play the games from previous levels. The more children read, the more confident and successful they will become as readers.

Don't panic!

Confident readers have times when they seem to be making progress and other times when they seem to be standing still. If you are anxious about your child's reading, ask their teacher for help.

Meanwhile:

- Try not to let your child see you are worried or they will become more anxious.

- Keep positive about what they are doing successfully. Offer lots of praise when they get things right.

- Suggest re-reading books they have already read and enjoyed. Challenge them to start using more expression when they re-read them.

- Spend time looking at other books and picture books. What else can you see in The Book People catalogue that your child might enjoy reading or listening to?

- Talk about books, play games, look carefully at pictures for details you might have missed last time round.

Questions parents often ask

When should I start reading with my child?

It's never too early. Babies and toddlers enjoy looking at picture books and hearing them read aloud. Chant nursery rhymes, sing songs and share picture books from birth onwards!

Should I teach my child the alphabet?

Yes. Teach the alphabet through songs and games, but focus more on letter sounds rather than names when you're doing reading activities. Encourage children to learn both letter names and letter sounds, with magnetic letters, and games like *I spy*.

What if my child is more interested in the pictures than the words?

In many early reading books, the pictures are much more interesting than the text! Continue to read stories to your child as they focus on the pictures. Most of the story-based activities in this Handbook concentrate on overall meaning and understanding, and can be taught through pictures. Focus on the words and letters through the word and phonics activities.

What should I do if they keep wanting the same book?

Don't discourage them. It's good to have favourite books, and reading familiar stories gives them confidence.

When and how can I ask my child to start trying to read with me?

Be guided by your child – don't force the pace too early or you risk putting them off. Re-read the advice on pages 8–12. If your child isn't ready, spend more time reading to them and playing games. If they're asking what words say, they're probably ready to begin. Start with a familiar story (for example, *Goldilocks*) with lots of repeated phrases. The *Read at Home* stories have lots of repetition and patterning.

What if my child makes a mistake while they're reading?

Don't stop the flow of the reading unless what they've read doesn't make sense. The meaning is the most important thing in reading in the early stages, and accuracy will come.

What should I do if they get stuck on a word?

In the early stages, quietly say the word. Later:

- encourage them to refer to the picture
- get them to try the first sound of the word
- break the word into chunks (syllables)
- get them to read the whole sentence and then ask them to guess the word. Focus on the meaning.

What if my child seems to stop making progress?

Don't worry. Children develop at different speeds and they always need to consolidate what they are learning before moving on. Continue to re-read familiar books, introduce new books at the same level, play the games and always be encouraging. Once they are ready, progress will resume.

Don't put pressure on them or you will spoil the fun!

Home—School Links

When your child starts school, continue to read to and with them as often as you can.

◈ Make use of home/school reading records to share your child's achievements and worries about reading.

◈ Talk to the teacher if you feel that a book is too hard or too easy for your child. There's usually a good reason why they've been given a particular book.

◈ Continue to wide range of books as well as you reading books. Use activities from this Handbook to extend your child's enjoyment of their reading book.

100 Common Useful Links used in the Read at Home stories

a, after, all, am, an, and, another, at, away, back, ball, been, began, big, but, can, can't, children, cold, come, could, Dad, didn't, do, dog, family, fast, find, for, get, go, going, good, got, had, has, he, help, here, him, his, I, in, is, it, just, know, like, look, looking, let's, make, me, Mum, must, my, need, no, not, of, on, out, over, play, pull, push, ran, said, saw, see, she, so, some, someone, something, stop, suddenly, surprise, take, that, the, them, they, there, this, thought, to, took, up, very, wants, was, we, went, were, what, where, with, yes, you

Useful Contacts offering advice on reading

Booktrust produces booklists and other information. www.booktrusted.co.uk
Tel: 020 8516 2977

British Dyslexia Association is the national organisation for specific learning difficulties. www.bda-dyslexia.org.uk
Tel: 0118 966 8271 (helpline)

Oxford University Press
Find out more about the *Oxford Reading Tree* at www.OxfordPrimary.com

The Parent Centre is the Department for Education and Skills website for all parents and carers. www.parentcentre.gov.uk

Reading is Fundamental is an initiative of the **National Literacy Trust** (www.literacytrust.org.uk).
RiF promotes reading for pleasure and offers parents advice and support.
www.rif.org.uk
Tel: 020 7828 2435

About Oxford Reading and Read at Home

Oxford Reading Tree

Oxford Reading Tree is used in over 80% of UK primary schools and helped millions of children learn to read around the world. *Oxford Tree* teachers realise the appeal of the characters in motivating chi̲ to want to learn to read, and they understand that reading s come̲ ̲s from working through the *Oxford Reading ̲ree* stages, which have bee̲ ̲ ̲ carefully ̲ ̲ support progression.

"We don't just like Oxford Reading Tree we LOVE it! We love it because it is simply the best reading scheme available! The stories are real stories about real people. The humour and vitality of the text and the illustrations engage children and adults alike making the reading experience a valued shared one ... These are real books. Real books, with the bonus of a unique structured approach to learning to read."

East Park Infant School, Wolverampton

About the Oxford Reading Tree author and illustrator

Author Roderick Hunt and Illustrator Alex Brychta, are two of the most experienced and successful reading scheme creators in the world. In 2008, Roderick Hunt received an MBE for services to education in the Queen's Birthday Honours List. This was followed by further success when Roderick and Alex won the prestigious Outstanding Achievement Award at the Education Resources Awards 2009.

Also from Read at Home

Flashcards and activities

Learn to read and have fun with word, picture and letter sound games.

6 flashcard sets available

Have fun with sticker activity books

16 stories available

First Experiences

Prepare your child for new situations like a visit to the dentist or their first day at school, in a fun and sensitive way.

First Skills

Learn and develop first skills through story.

8 stories available

10 stories available

Floppy's Phonics

Floppy's Phonics enables children to practise their letters and sounds at home.

OXFORD
UNIVERSITY PRESS

Great Clarendon Street, Oxford OX2 6DP

Oxford is a registered trade mark of Oxford University Press
in the UK and in certain other countries

Acknowledgements

Text © Kate Ruttle and Annemarie Young 2005
Illustrations © Alex Brychta 2005
The moral rights of the author/artist have been asserted

The publisher would like to thank the following for permission to reproduce
photographs: **p7** Apollofoto/Shutterstock.com; **p25** Rarpia/iStock

Database right Oxford University Press (maker)
First published 2005
This edition published 2010

ISBN 978 0 19 838780 0

10 9 8 7 6 5 4 3 2 1
Printed in China by Imago
www.oup.com
Paper used in the production of this book is a natural, recyclable product
made from wood grown in sustainable forests. The manufacturing process
conforms to the environmental regulations of the country of origin.